Ronin

Mostly Prose Poems

Paul Juhasz

Fine Dog Press

For Jeanetta Calhoun Mish,
O Captain! My Captain!

> "We are the hollow men
> We are the stuffed men
> Leaning together
> Headpiece filled with straw."
> T.S. Eliot

CONTENTS

Ripples 1

The Relevance of Cathedrals

Storm's Coming 4

While Notre Dame Burned 5

Best in Show 7

Hill Country 8

Salad 10

Pantoum for a Father 12

Menagerie 14

Butterfly Effect 16

His Way 18

CONTENTS

▎Blaze of Glory: An Ode to Byron, Who was a Good Cat, But Unfortunately Had to Die 20

▎Why I Was Late to Your Reading 22

▎Another Sunny Day 24

▎Upon Visiting the National World War I Museum 25

▎A Postcard from the Edge 27

▎Squawk Box at the Rio Gorge Bridge 28

Crying on the Inside

▎Tips for a Happy and Healthy Life (2019 Edition) 32

▎Visiting Fort Wagner 34

▎Gone 36

▎This Poem is Not About My Father 37

▎Scar Stories 41

CONTENTS

At the Oklahoma Department of Public Safety 45

At the Funeral of Peter's Father 46

A New Experience? 48

There and Back Again 49

The Sky is Crying 50

Birthday Wish 51

Lovelorn 53

The Hare Licks His Wounds 55

Nightmare 57

The Problem with Inspiration 59

This Life Instead Of

Ronin 62

Hermit 64

Coward 65

Eighth Ring 68

CONTENTS

They Wave as They Drive By 69

Seven Tips for Uber-Riders: A Helpful Guide 70

Masturbators 74

I Was Trying to Write a Poem 76

I, Sherrett 80

Pulling Weeds 82

Beard 84

Bartholomew Cubbins Tries Psychoanalysis 86

Barn Cat 88

Because I'm A White Man 89

Just Missed 92

Beautifully, Impossibly, In Flight

Vectors 96

Not All Who Wander Are Lost 98

CONTENTS

- Essential Oils 100
- He Prefers Not To 102
- Usually 104
- This is Just to Say Something Else 106
- Residue 107
- Wisdom 108
- The Last Glove I Will Ever Buy 109
- Wisdom, Continued 111
- Paper Thin 113
- Cocoon 115
- Gestalt 116
- Oklahoma, Considered 117
- First Lines 119
- Amazing Hot Dogs 121
- Bucket List 123

CONTENTS

▎How to Write an Oklahoma Poem 126

Unfettered by Ephemeral Fears

▎Exodus 130

▎Acknowledgments 132

ABOUT THE AUTHOR 137

Ronin

Ripples

A ronin limps to the edge of the lake. The wound in his side, taut and caked now, threatens to pull at each step. Behind him the crows have found the battlefield and the slow, savoring, clean-up has begun. Soon the dogs will arrive for their grand share. Slowly, stiffly, he lowers himself onto a rock. A crane stands at a distant shore-edge, bill poised, waiting, watching, waiting. Wincing, the ronin tosses a pebble into the pellucid before him, considers the ripples. A sunset, the susurrus of frogs, the sound of water, and a ronin, wanderer, wave-man, idlily fondling the green weave of his tantō handle, deep in thought, deep in thought.

The Relevance of Cathedrals

Storm's Coming

Storm's coming.
Dark clouds straddle the horizon, boiling with menace.
roiling forward like clenched fists,
each larger and darker than the one before it.
Lighting flashing at its fringes, the clouds churn.
Oranges, pinks, yellows, and purples,
grumbling, growling, growing.
Some aren't concerned.
To them, the clouds are just a photo opportunity,
part of a lovely landscape.
They don't see what I see:
Storm's coming.
And it'll be here soon.

While Notre Dame Burned

While Notre Dame burned, thousands of people rushed to Facebook to post photos of themselves posed in front of the cathedral, with profound statements of sorrow, such as "so sad" or "OMG. Frowny face." A woman told her friend on the phone, "Well, at least I got to see it." An American xenophobe sat at his dinner table, telling his children about the prevalence of pickpockets. Disney's *Captain Marvel* broke the $1 billion mark in gross sales. Burger King brought back the Angry Whopper to satisfy popular demand. A tourist in Tokyo bravely orders *fugu*. A father tells his son he had a dream he was a muffler, woke up exhausted.

While Notre Dame burned, an eight-foot alligator walked into a Florida Wal-Mart. Three Mashco Piros pin-cushioned a lost logger stumbling through the Amazon undergrowth. An emperor penguin coddled a precious egg on its feet. A seventy-five-year-old man was killed by his pet cassowary. A klipspringer skipped across rock and scrub, delighting in the musical name it's been given. An asteroid continued through deep space on a planet-killing vector.

While Notre Dame burned, as its spire and roof collapsed inward, a homeless man hopes that the facilities at Alton Park are unlocked, so he could complete his morning ablutions and once again fade from notice. A busboy in San Antonio is torn between worry over a wall and the scandal of casually-wasted food. A man in the backseat of an Uber laughs into his phone, "I'll knock her up just for the tittie-fucking." An ex-father is charged with attempted homicide for throwing a young boy off a balcony at the Mall of America. An obscure poet puts down his Whitman and opens his laptop; as the cursor winks at him, he ponders the relevance of cathedrals, the faintest whisper of a fiddle in his ear.

Best in Show

Sister was for show:
lip stick and rouge, car rides, dance tracks, entry fees
Business attire, bathing suit (dry), evening wear,
                                    Ms. Congeniality
In the end, we meant well.
But not everyone gets a trophy.
Sister was for show.

Hill Country

The town keeps expanding, consuming. Like a virus or a weed. Pushing ever outward, in all directions at once. Mindless and inexorable. The ranchers on the fringe complain about the townsfolk, calling them a cancer, a threat to their way of life, as they toss the carcass of a slain coyote across their barbed wire fence.

If asked about this, they explain this practice warns other coyotes to stay away. I don't know what I find funnier: the fact that these ranchers think this actually works, or the image their belief calls to mind. A bunch of coyotes standing around, perhaps holding steaming cups of coffee before their shift or ice-cold bottles of Corona at the end of one, then one coyote saying to the others, "Hey, you hear what happened to Phil? Rancher Johnson caught him on his land, shot him dead. Hung Phil's body on the fence. We best stay out of Rancher Johnson's pasture if you ask me." The other coyotes then nod at the sagacity of such advice. Perhaps one mumbles some-thing about that being a damn shame. Perhaps he says this not because he liked Phil, but because Phil owed him some money. I'll laugh at this too, because coyotes have no pockets. Where would they keep something as essential as money with-out pockets? They're not kangaroos, after all.

Meanwhile, as the ranchers drape their wire boundaries with the corpses of apex predators, those same townsfolk they complain of—when they take breaks from complaining about the jackrabbits running unfettered over their land—those same townsfolk are posting on the Facebook stories about finding mountain lion tracks across their manicured back lawns, about the latest black bear or rattlesnake sighting. They'll be shocked and alarmed at the menace encroaching on their sterilized, hermetically-sealed lives. They wonder if perhaps the ranchers have the right idea, ponder where they could hang a dead cougar or bear on their property. The mailbox, perhaps, or maybe the door-knocker. Then they'll sip their chamomile or their Scotch, secure in their belief that the snake always rattles before it strikes.

Salad

The consensus was that the cucumber was a mistake.

A shame, really. They had been working together so well for so long. Sure, early on there was the incident with Moses, his insistence that they use Romaine lettuce. His self-righteous cries that Iceberg had no real nutritional value, his outlandish idea of a dressing made with anchovy paste. But they handled that. Told Mo to get his own damn kitchen where he could make all the crazy salads he wanted to. Hell, he could even throw grilled chicken, or salmon, or shrimp (well, maybe not shrimp) on it if he wanted to. It was no longer any of their concern.

But then Mary had to suggest the cucumber.

Martin objected first. "The cucumber," he yelled, "is nothing but a cylinder of water. It lacks any real substance."

Cal insisted that he and he alone could make decisions on ingredients, and he loathed the cucumber. Although, to be fair, while Cal believed the cucumber was a particularly odious vegetable, all vegetables, coming as they did from dirt and shit, were inherently depraved. No amount of washing, Cal was convinced, could make them clean.

"That's irrelevant," John contended. "What *is* relevant is that cucumber was not on the original list of ingredients. As such, it cannot be used. We can't just let anyone, not even you, Cal, and certainly not Mary, add ingredients to the list as they wish. Before you know it, we'd have quinoa on our salads, for God's sake!"

"It looks like a phallus," Jim argued. His wife had already left the room in tears, blue mascara melting down her cheeks, after Charles—Godless man—used the phrase "salad tossing."

"Sladbab bwananana pffffit," Jones babbled over his shoulder at them all, before resuming his fondling of the butcher's twine while contemplating Kool-Aid.

Outside, the masses: some seated on logs, some on rocks, most on the cool, damp ground. Waiting. Wondering when dinner would be served.

Pantoum for a Father

His affection was peculiar.
Wash certain parts more than once.
Lather it up again.
What a nice cock!

Wash certain parts more than once.
Swinging parties pool-side.
What a nice cock!
Porn-tapes paused mid-scene.

Swinging parties pool-side.
No one will believe this.
Porn-tapes paused mid-scene.
Cherish the money shot.

No one will believe it.
Doors must not be locked.
Cherish the money-shot.
Insertion up to the second knuckle.

RONIN

Doors must not be locked.
Lather it up again.
Insertion up to the second knuckle.
His affection was peculiar.

Menagerie

It caused a bit of a stir when the townspeople awoke one April morning to find that they were all hermit crabs. There was some initial grumbling that all the good shells were taken (and the town drunk opted for no shell at all, curling his tapering abdomen around the park bench under which he routinely slept), but the grousing eventually passed, just has it did in March when they had all been changed into impalas, and as it had in February, when they were Komodo dragons.

Predictably, cults soon appeared. One that looked forward to the time when the townspeople would be penguins, at peace with their ridiculous wobbling. The other hankered for a return to the days when all were kangaroos, days of athletic travel and carrying things with ease.

In the park, the town sage called for an assembly. "These changes," he declared, "are parables. They are meant to be instructive. That month we were camels we were supposed to learn how to ration, to budget. The month we were crows, to expand our horizons, to see new places."

"But no one went anywhere," a small crab nestled in a periwinkle shell called out.

"And what about that time we were octopuses," a large crab who had moved into what looked suspiciously like a Skoal tin said. "We suddenly had four times as many hands as we were used to. Had no idea what to do with them. It was chaos. Anarchy."

A crab peeking out of a painted shell, peace symbol on one side, smiley face on the other, asked. "Isn't anyone going to ask the obvious question? Why do we keep changing?"

"No!" several crabs shouted.

"And," Skoal-tin crab yelled at the town sage, "if you're so smart, perhaps you'd care to explain what that shit with the hyraxes was all about."

"Yeah," another joined. "I didn't even know there was such a thing as a hyrax, 'til we turned into them."

The town sage was silent, for he also had no idea about the hyrax thing. Misinterpreting his silence for the end of the assembly, the crowd scuttled off, some plodding under the unaccustomed weight of their shell homes, others trying to master their pinchers. The one thing the town agreed upon (except for the now-despondent sage) was that the shells and pinchers were an improvement. But how and over what, no one could really say.

Butterfly Effect

She strokes the revolver lovingly, its gun-metal-blue steel mirroring the bruises and welts that dapple her arms and back, a gift from two days ago, when dinner was not on the table when Bob got home from work.

Elie Mae Hooper cannot know that in a few short months, after spending the afternoon drinking in a hotel bar, she will meet Richard Speck, an obscure criminal about to hit the bigtime. Cannot know that, gun or not, he will force Elie Mae into his hotel room and repeatedly rape her. Cannot know that when he is finished with her he'll go visit Chicago's Jeffery Manor neighborhood, where he will spend the night stabbing, strangling, and raping eight nursing students.

All she knows is that before any of this happens, the gun makes her feel safe, makes Bob leave the house the one time she shows it to him, slows his rage in the weeks that follow.

In the TimeLife book on American Crime in which my son reads of Speck's gruesome murders, an anonymous author writes:

> "using Elie Mae Hooper's handgun,
> Speck forced his way into the townhouse."

As my son reads, a butterfly flaps its wings in our backyard.

His Way

He flew down the stairs,
draped only in a towel,
stillborn shower beaded his shoulders,
cascaded down his greasy, not-washed hair.

"What the fuck is this," he said,
pointing at the speakers
as if a physical manifestation of the song
had oozed forth.

"Um, it's Sinatra." I answered,
a bit startled that he did not know
who had been belting out "My Way"
a few moments before.

"I know it's Sinatra. But why are *you* listening to it."
"Why shouldn't I listen to it?"
"Because that's not your music.
It's mine."

By this time in my life,
I understood my father was incapable
of being ironic,
so I said nothing to this.

"Play something else" he demanded,
then pivoted back up the stairs,
to wash away the dirt and grime
he thought was only skin deep.

Blaze of Glory: An Ode to Byron, Who was a Good Cat, But Unfortunately Had to Die

When you had your second stroke in a week, we knew the forty-minute drive to the vet in your condition would be cruel and needless, so it was decided I would take you out back and end your misery.

The first shot was to put you down.

Shots two, three, four, and five were because you started twitching. I panicked and thought the first, carefully aimed shot hadn't done the trick.

Shots six, seven, and eight were because I was angry. Angry with you for dying. Angry that I, a life-long dog person, had to admit I gave a shit.

Shots nine, ten, and eleven were because I was pretending I was in a Western, squeezing off hip-shots like Steve McQueen, winging imaginary desperados and assorted bad guys (all of which, of course, were just you. Or what was once you).

Shots twelve, thirteen, fourteen, and fifteen were because the recoil of the rifle started to remind me of sex. The polished walnut grip a stand-in for sensuously-bucking, deeply-tanned flesh.

Shots sixteen, seventeen, and eighteen were because I knew the Marlin .22 held eighteen shots in its magazine, and I saw no reason to go back to the garage with those three held back.

So, thanks for the memories, Byron. You were a good cat. I will miss you.

And I hope that when my time comes, I shall go out in a similar blaze of glory. Unless, by then, we have come up with something we value even more.

Why I Was Late to Your Reading

I was making great time until I came across the body on the road.

It lay in state, perpendicular to the double-yellow line. Dirty Carhart jacket, faded jeans, tattered socks, no shoes. The face of the body on the road was serene, almost beatific. There was no blood, there no movement. There was just a body on the road.

No one seemed too concerned about the body on the road. Not the driver of the white pick-up coming the other way. He just slowed a bit, swerved onto the shoulder, giving the body on the road the most cursory of glances.

Not the 911 operator I called. Nor the second operator to whom she transferred me. Nor the third. Nor the fourth. What all four 911 operators *were* concerned about was the county I was calling from. Each pressed me for that information. Paperwork is important, I guess.

None of them wanted to hear about the body on the road. I hung up on the fourth operator, sensing my call was inconvenient, the body on the road irrelevant.

And that's why I was late to your reading, arriving just as you began your last poem, the one about that time a hitchhiker tried to rob you while his son cried in the backseat. You willingly gave the man your money and the groceries you just bought as well, drove them to local hotel and put three nights on your credit card. You end that poem wondering what happened to the hitchhiker and his boy.

    I wondered in turn what happened to your audience. Most of the chairs in the cavernous gallery sat empty and neglected, your words swallowed by the hollow din of apathy. I guess people weren't concerned about your poetry. They didn't want to hear about the hitchhiker and his boy. They thought they had better things to do.

Another Sunny Day

When the leaves of the pineapples on my Hawaiian shirt start to grow, they tickle at first, but as the shirt continues to fray and dissolve, the waxy greens scratch and rub raw. Soon, there is no shirt at all, just green spikes that stab and tear, that pierce, draining juice into the glass my father will drink for breakfast as he reads his newspaper and contemplates how he will spend this gloriously perfect day.

Upon Visiting the National World War I Museum

People shuffle through room upon room filled with tools of Death,
Their eyes glazed over as they read of the buildup and the causes:
Being told of an exponential advance of technology,
      of dreams of Empire,
      of a lust for land,
      of wealth concentrated in the hands of a few,
      of the rise of nationalism,
      of divisions based on ethnic and racial identity.
      We are us, they are them.

And then a spark, and thirty-eight million bodies consumed in the blaze.

A woman pretends to read the placard in the case before her,
while eyeballing the dark-skinned man to her left.
She is convinced he has a bomb and is about to kill us all.
She does not understand that India is not in the Middle East,
and it probably would not matter if she did.
Dark skin is dark skin.

PAUL JUHASZ

We are us, they are them.

A man with a red hat declaring yellow promises sadly shakes his head in front of a bayonet
display, wonders how men could do such things to each other.
Tonight, he'll watch clear and balanced news, and pray we shove a nuke straight up Kim-Jong
Un's ass.

In a soundproof room, Wilfred Owen
tells us *"dulce et decorum est pro patria mori"*
is bullshit propaganda.
But the room is empty

Above the museum stands Liberty Tower, visibility ten miles on a clear day.
The visibility inside the museum remains zero, no matter the weather.
I make my way to the exit,
alongside the doomed shuffling outside,
To await the coming spark.

A Postcard from the Edge

I'm supposed to write "Wish you were here," but that's just one of those courteous lies we're trained to tell. I don't wish you were here. I really don't. But please don't take that hard, don't be offended. The "you" is not *just* you; I don't wish anyone was here. And where "here" is, doesn't really matter, either. Which is why this "postcard" is merely a white 3x5 index card. "Here" can be anywhere, is everywhere.

Wish you were here.

Wish you were

Wish you

Wish

Squawk Box at the Rio Gorge Bridge

It spans across the Rio Grande Gorge, ten miles west of Taos on U.S. Rt 64. One of the highest bridges in the country, yet it sneaks up on you, both the bridge and the gorge not apparent until you are right on top of them, the marvel of the bridge only something observable in photos or from a rest area just west of the gorge. Neither the bridge, the rest area, nor the gorge are noted by immediate highway signage, so you don't know to stop and look until the moment you're crossing. Then, you either have to turn around or stop and park on the bridge itself (ignoring the No Parking signs like everyone else). Even then, your perspective is limited to a top-down view.

But, oh, that perspective. More than six hundred feet down to a snake of a river, too palsied and weak, it seems from up here, to have created such a striking wound in the earth. You're so high up, turkey vultures vector below you on the warm air currents trapped between jagged rock, brown as old scabs ready to flake.

Since its completion in 1965, there have been hundreds of documented suicides, a fact exposed by the square box near one of the overlooks. With the press of a button, a would-be jumper can communicate with a prevention hotline. The box looks old and neglected, painted a cold blue. Where the paint has flaked off, a hard steel glares out from behind rust's edge.

The box makes me think of the hundreds of screws-up I've experienced at hundreds of fast food restaurants, a garbled, mechanical, inhuman voice failing to comprehend something as simple as my desire to have them "hold the mayo, please." I think of misheard dipping sauces and partial orders lost in depersonalized transmission, and I think of the last jumper here, silhouetted by the piercing rays of sunset that render sunglasses useless, and I wonder that here, at the edge of experience, at the threshold of pain and alienation, within one's last moments, is this truly the best we can do?

Crying on the Inside

Tips for a Happy and Healthy Life (2019 Edition)

Eat fruit. On time is five minutes late. If you are fat, be funny (see: Candy, John; McCarthy, Melissa). Surface is everything. Do not block the box. Objects in mirror are closer than they appear. Historical marker ahead. Take care of yourself; your labor is important. Can you measure your pain on a scale of zero (no pain) to ten (the worst pain imaginable)? In the event of an actual emergency, your seat cushion can be used as a floatation device. If you are good-looking, please be quiet—you are to be easy on the eyes, not the ears. Surface is everything. In case of emergency, break glass. Abraham Maslow's hierarchy is a valuable reference, but please keep in mind he only lived to sixty-two. Drink between eight to twelve cups of water a day. This is not a life-saving device. Yield to oncoming traffic. None of this is about you. Yogurt is the new caviar. No flash photography. Practice your "O" face. Surface is everything. Consumption is vital to the machine. We are not responsible for stolen, lost, or damaged items. Reserved for Employee-of-the-Month. Living well is the best revenge, but decapitation is a close second. If you are neither fat nor good-looking, you may speak if you validate what we think. Surface is everything. Where there's smoke, there's fire. Take two tablets every six hours as needed. When they ask, "What kind of clown are you?" do not reply: "the crying on the inside kind." Surface is everything.

Visiting Fort Wagner

There are no parking lots.
You have to park in a residential *cul-de-sac*
and walk a half mile to the beach.

There are no gift shops.
Consider: even Walden Pond has a gift shop.

There's not even a placard.
Actually, there is one: about local shorebirds and their nests.
I was prepared for the fact that Morris Island and the site of
    the fort is under water,
the Atlantic filling in for Sandburg's grass,
whitewashing the landscape of the heroic and the horrible.

But I was not prepared for the nothingness.
nothing that celebrates, indicates, fabricates,
nothing that breathes what happened here.

Nothing of Robert Gould Shaw or the 54th Massachusetts.
Nothing of their brave assault on the Confederate fort.
Nothing of the proof, clear and incontrovertible, that all men
    were created equal,
that black lives do indeed matter.

Shaw's parents said of the mass grave here,
where Shaw was buried to the mocking delight
of Confederate victors ("with his niggers," they laughed),
that there was "no holier place" for their son to be.

But this holy place is now under forty feet of ocean water,
near a narrow, unmarked stretch of sand.
Erased from the landscape by Nature,
and from our minds by choice.

As I sit on a rock and ponder this erasure, this void,
a man approaches, several cotton T-shirts slung over his shoulder.
He asks if I'd like to buy one.
"To save the lighthouse," he adds, pointing to a thin strip of land jutting into the
water at the end of which stands a frail, lonely, desolate structure,
intended to guide a people who no longer come for guidance.

"You're too late, brother." I reply. "The lighthouse is already gone."

Gone

It sits in the corner of the garage,
dust levelling the orange dimples.
A scripted Wilson folded in on itself,
like the toothless gums of an old man.
Sits, half-deflated,
neglected, ignored,
waiting, hoping, to be played with
again.

This Poem is Not About My Father

Let me make one thing perfectly clear: This poem is *not* about my father. I've been told that too much I write is about my father, that I'm a one-trick pony, and I should stop going to the well too often, whatever the hell that means. So, there will be no wells nor ponies doing tricks of any kind in this poem, which is *not* about my father.

I was originally going to write a poem about how I do not like any of my father's sports teams (which is, of course, not *technically* a poem about my father) How as a young boy I began, without any clear perception of what I was doing, to pull for the bitter rivals of my father's favorite teams. My Flyers and Phillies vs. his Rangers and Mets. About how those allegiances have held up for more than forty years. "This," I said to myself, "would make an interesting topic for a poem." But it will not be *this* poem. Because this poem is *not* about my father.

Maybe I should write a poem about a boy who finds a magical gemstone, one that can transport him to a wonderful world of cotton candy clouds and billboards that challenge the moral assumptions of orthodontia. Or maybe to a place where the boy could freely laugh at the kumquat, could dine on cake that is mostly frosting, or at the very least, have a very flavorful muffin. Or perhaps there could be a troll there, a troll that wanted to be good but was bad by accident. Or even better, hippogriffs. Yeah, there should be hippogriffs. Hippogriffs are cool. All of those, I believe, would be better poems than a poem about my father.

I have been told I have "Daddy Issues." I always smile when people say this, because I have written a short story called "Daddy Issues." It's about a support group this guy joins. A lot of other people with Daddy Issues are in this group. Hamlet is in it. Luke Skywalker is in it. So is Jesus. Harry Chapin has a bit part in the story. None of these characters, however, will appear in *this* poem, none of them will laugh at the kumquat or eat frosting, because this poem is *not* about my father.

Because this poem is *not* about my father, there will be no mention of being abandoned at a Connecticut state park when I was eight because my father thought it would be funny, no mention of the numbing terror I experienced, no skillfully-selected word choice to express what my screams and cries were like. For example, there will be no mention of wounded animals (not even of hippogriffs), nor will words like "primal" or "atavistic" be used. Nor the phrase "trust issues." I solemnly vow that the phrase "trust issues" will *not* appear in this poem.

Because this poem is *not* about my father, I will make no mention of the beating at Disney World, nor the one for being friends with a black kid in junior high, nor will the topic of my father turning a blind eye to my sister's insanity, even after she stabbed me, even after my father discovered six Rubbermaid totes full of used tampons she was collecting, dating, and naming (names like "Carl," "Charlie," and "Alexander," which are *silly* names for tampons), even after she held a loaded gun to my head, said she was going to kill me if I didn't leave the house. There will be no mention of me leaving the house. Because this poem is *not* about my father, there will be no mention of how he'd stick his head behind the curtain when I showered, charting my growth, reminding me to wash certain parts more than once, nor of how my own sons do not feel comfortable around him.

There will no exploration of how—or even if—I envy men my age who have functional, perhaps even rewarding, relationships with their fathers. Who perhaps even exchange gemstones with them. I will not make analogies to amputees, nor use the phrase "phantom pain" in any way. Nor shall I explore whether I am sad about my lack of a relationship with my father or sad that I'm not sad about it. Such explorations have no place here, for this poem is *not* about my father.

I also will not discuss how I have this near-paralyzing fear that I will make all of the same mistakes; that I will become him. Because I always dismiss these fears. It is unlikely I will become like my father, for my father never wrote a poem about his relationship with his father. I feel better after I realize this, safe in the knowledge that I will not make those same mistakes, that I'll make completely different mistakes. However, none of these topics, I solemnly swear, will appear in this poem. You have my word. Because this poem is certainly, most definitely, unequivocally *not* about my father.

This poem is about a boy and a magical gemstone, heavily-frosted cake, and, if all goes well, a hippogriff.

Scar Stories

Perhaps inspired by that scene in *Jaws*, where Quint and Hooper compare scars and swap stories, my son wants to talk about scars, my scars.

He points to the faded line on my left breast first. "Kicked up a rock with a lawn mower when I was about your age," I tell him. "Imagine if it hit just a little bit higher. Could have lost an eye. *That's* why I harp on you to wear eye-protection when you mow."

Your Aunt Susan stabbed me there with a pair of scissors, when I was about your age. Sure, it hurt, but not as much as your grandfather deciding to pretend it didn't happen, not as much as him choosing her over me.

"This line on my finger? A whittling accident. Wasn't careful enough with my first pocketknife. That's why I'm always on you about yours, how when you're using it, that is the only thing in the world worth your attention."

Your great-grandmother did not like how I was cutting the pork roll for breakfast. Was making the slices too

> *thick. So, she grabbed my hand and twisted it. When the knife slipped, it sliced into my hand. She said I was just being a baby, that it wasn't deep enough for stitches.*

"That one on my shoulder? I was riding a toy firetruck around my father's pool table when I lost control and cut my shoulder on one of the metal edges. Needed ten stitches to close it up. That's why I keep telling you not to run around the house. You can trip and hit something, and really hurt yourself."

> *There really wasn't a firetruck. Just a drunk mother who decided I was in the way.*

"You want to hear the story about my tongue again? I bit through it playing basketball. The guy I was guarding went up for a shot, his shoulder crashed into my jaw. Almost bit it clean off, only about an inch or two left holding it together. And, man, did it bleed. Took more than a hundred stitches to sew it back together. Didn't eat solid food for three weeks. And that's why you got to wear a mouth guard."

> *Your grandfather didn't like the way I answered him one night. I was sweet on this girl, Eileen Butterfield, and your grandfather had this weird thing about*

my penis. Always asking to see it, making sure it was washed extra good when I showered. So he says to me that night, "You don't need some bitch in heat to tell you you have a nice dick; that's my job." Which was an odd thing for a father to say to a son. And I told him that.

Your grandfather usually went with the jab, upon occasion the roundhouse, but this was the first time he went with the uppercut, so I never saw it coming. Imagine if my teeth were just a little bit better at meeting, who would tell you those dad jokes that make you groan? Who would tell you that the world is supposed to be a happy place? Who would tell you false stories about scars?

"Those circles on my hand? Well, they look like bubbles, but they're really burns. I was cooking Chinese food and apparently had the wok too hot. When I added the sesame oil, it splattered all over the place, including on my hand."

I did those burns myself. With cigarettes. When I was in college. As punishment.

And here's the weird thing: I still feel the urge to do it every day. Every. Single. Day. Sometimes, when I'm enjoying a nice cigar with "Uncle" Hank, all I can think about is how long until he goes and takes a piss so I can press the ash into my flesh, hear it sizzle.

"Scars add character, son. Scars are proof of healing."

And every day the void whispers to me:

You deserve it.

At the Oklahoma Department of Public Safety

As I sit waiting for my number to be called, permission to exchange this large institutional room for a smaller one, I think of all the ways this can go wrong:

What if the required documentation listed on the website was incorrect? What if my birth certificate is not official enough? Can they reject my identity? Will they throw me out?

What if I fail the eye test? I can't read that license plate on the other side of the parking lot, so surely I'm doomed. If I can't pass, am I still allowed to drive home?

Will coffee help? Or will it just make me jittery? If I get jittery, will the security guard think I'm on meth? They execute meth heads in Oklahoma, don't they?

Goddamn it, all I want is to transfer my out-of-state driver's license!

My breaths become short. Forced. Panicked.

There are palpitations.

I am forced to face an existential truth:

I have read too much Kakfa.

At the Funeral of Peter's Father

The images flashing across the TV screens show a tall, blockish, athletic man, a far cry from the worn husk I recall shuffling from parking lots toward bleachers, the journey costing you two innings. I always assumed you were Peter's grandfather, so wasted and sucked dry by cancer were you. Over the course of the season, we exchanged maybe two or three head nods, the barest minimum of human recognition, nothing more than noting shared general interest, about what you'd give to someone in a museum sharing a glance at the same artifact, reading the same placard. As I shuffle past your closed casket, it occurs to me that I never even knew your name, would still not know it if it wasn't printed on the prayer card the funeral director hands out at the door.

So, then, how do I connect with you? How do I find my way into this experience? To make it profound and meaningful? To honor you and celebrate that you lived a life, made some difference? To justify my being here with you at the end?

I see a giant floral bouquet sent by the New York Giants, so clearly you were a football fan. Is that enough? I mean, to be a football fan in America is hardy unique. And I have always hated the Giants.

The prayer card also informs me you were just three years older than me. Is that it, then? A generational connection? But how to embrace that without reducing your death to my own *momento mori*, without making all this about me?

Peter's handshake in the receiving line reminds me that you were a father, so maybe that's it. But there are billions of fathers, and I have no way, now, to know if you were a good one or not. An artificial narrative, no matter how soothing or how cleverly-crafted, is not connection.

Ultimately, all I can offer you, Stephen, is the simple acknowledgment that you were once here. Is that enough?

As the precession line trickles to an end, Peter is surrounded by all of his teammates, eleven boys, my son among them, smiling, slapping each other on shoulder and hand, talking of vital irrelevancies with wonder. Their grins and laughs promise the next game, and I leave the room for the porch outside where the parents have gathered, stepping out into our great shared shame.

A New Experience?

We were about 200 miles outside of Memphis when you got hungry, wanted to pull off at the next exit. You looked at the blue highway sign as it flashed by and said Jeff's Shrimp and Things sounded good.

We pulled off, dutifully took the left turn the follow-up sign directed and looked at the marquee: Johnny's Steak and Seafood.

And I laughed and laughed, because you really didn't get *any* of it right, did you? A moment of strained silence followed, as you tried to decide whether to be insulted. Then it passed and we laughed together this time.

Because there was really no chance we were eating there anyway.

There and Back Again

In any journey narrative, with the exception of Homer's *The Odyssey* (which, of course, is *all* Back Again), the There is always more interesting than the Back Again.

The There is new and full of wonder. Who will be There? What will There be like? What will happen There? Will they have free WiFi, There? Or majestic vistas? Homemade pot pies?

There are no such hopes for Back Again. We know who is at Back Again, for we left them there. There is no need to speculate about what happens at the end of Back Again. At the end of Back Again are home repairs, screaming children, PTA meetings, and annoying co-workers. The pot pies are store-bought; the WiFi bundled into the cable bill.

Even the scenery is transformed in the interval between There and Back Again. There is full of "Wow! Look at that!" While Back Again is "Are we here already?"

The stay at There is never long enough to satisfy the anticipation, and the Back Again always confirms our dread.

Are we There yet?

The Sky is Crying

Storm clouds float across
Red-stained evening sky, leaving
Tears on moss-draped rocks.
As I sit alone, in a house meant for two.

Birthday Wish

They never come true anyway, but I suppose that's mostly my fault. I tend to make ill-considered requests.

When I was a child, they'd be wildly unrealistic. The unicorn I wished for when I was four, for example. Or my wish to be the owner/operator of a successful hyena farm, when I was nine. Stupid, really. I mean, the overhead alone!

When I hit my teen years, I decided to spit in the birthday wish's eye, to dare it to come true. The wishes became more absurd with each year. To make gumbo with Peter Boyle, to write a hippopotamus opera.

As I grew older, I tried to attach these birthday wishes onto social causes, a wish for justice, a universal response to global warming or world hunger, until I realized these wishes were just as absurd and unrealistic as wanting a unicorn or hippos singing *La Bohème*.

When my son came home from school last year, devastated by the knowledge that some day in the future, our sun will exhaust its fuel and it, the universe of which it is the center, and all life that we know of, will be extinguished, I used my wish to hope that wouldn't happen, or if it did have to happen, then that it wouldn't happen in his lifetime, or if it did have to happen in his lifetime, that he would find peace with himself before it did. I realize now that I made three wishes, and we're talking birthdays here, not lamps with genies, so I fucked that one up as well.

But this year, my birthday wish doesn't seem as unrealistic or as absurd as all the others. My wish depends on only one thing; a single person, making a single decision, to say three words And why not? I reason. Why can't this one wish, which doesn't involve hyena farms, or Peter Boyle, or operas of any kind, why can't *this* one come true?

The candles before me await the ceremony. I breath in, and wish, and blow.

I'll wait
and dream
and hope,
while the candle smokes,
extinguished.

Lovelorn

9:31 p.m.: Did I remember to turn the oven off?

9:57 p.m.: Should I get a fade? Perhaps an undercut? A mullet? Which would look best?

10:13 p.m.: If I fall asleep right now, I'll get 7 hours and 47 minutes.

10:24 p.m.: Did I lock the front door?

10:46 p.m.: Is Andy Dick still alive? How is that possible?

11:06 p.m.: What was that noise?

11:17 p.m.: Brexit. Discuss.

12:03 a.m.: Did I set the coffee-maker?

12:25 a.m.: If I fall asleep right now, I'll get 5 hours and 35 minutes.

12:39 a.m.: What should I wear? Was the green shirt her favorite? Or the purple?

1:00 a.m.: If they don't move, why are they called polka dots?

1:18 a.m.: Was that a creak on the steps?

1:19 a.m.: Who's there!?!

1:24 a.m.: Did I start the dishwasher?

1:26 a.m.: Do I have a dishwasher?

1:37 a.m.: I really hate the neighbor's cat. Not a fan of the dog either.

2:13 a.m.: How the fuck did Trump win!?!

2:25: a.m.: What if he does again?

2:31 a.m.: 1, 2, 3, 4, 5, 6, 7, 8, 9, 10.

2:33 a.m.: Fucking sheep!

2:59 a.m.: Can it be possible? If so, how? Why?

3:18 a.m.: What *was* the name of our mailman? McSorley? Mc Sweeny? Jones?

3: 33 a.m.: If I fall asleep right now, I'll get 2 hours and 27 minutes.

3:52 a.m.: Is that a lump?

4:20 a.m.: Rooster seems early.

4:46 a.m.: Aren't eggs boneless chicken?

5:02 a.m.: Fuck! Should I just get up?

5:15 a.m.: 45 minutes, that's like a solid nap, right?

5:32 a.m.: I should have just binge-watched *The Office*.

5:59 a.m.: What if she meant none of it?

The Hare Licks His Wounds

What no one understands, baby doll, is that I threw that first match. Do you really think I'd lose to a goddamn turtle? Fuck no, I threw that motherfucker! Why? Gotta generate interest. Build the excitement, baby. I mean, c'mon. Who was paying attention to that first race anyway? Friends and family, mostly. Wasn't any buzz. No juice, baby. It's all about the juice. So, like I said, gotta build the interest. Get demand up for a rematch. I'm nothing if not a show-man. This will be like Rocky-Apollo II, but better, 'cause I'll be in it. I'm also gonna let you in on a little secret; not too many people know this, but I made a pre-race call to Vegas last time. They had that tortoise a 20-1 underdog. Shit, baby, I know a good thing when I see it. That's why I'm talking to you. I made myself a cool twenty grand. So, you know I can take care of you tonight, baby doll, show you the sights, get you whatever you want. Gonna tell you something else; this time, it's in the bag. Got me an angle. No, not gonna cheat, take short cuts, anything like that. Even though I suspect that slow-ass motherfucker pulled some shit like that last time. No, nothing like that. This time, I'm calling in a favor. Got me Glenn Close on speed dial.

PAUL JUHASZ

She owes me, for what she did to Uncle Whitey in *Fatal Attraction*. And I've been filling her ears about the sweetness of mock turtle soup for days now, but, you know, without all that "mock" jazz. You gotta keep it real, baby. That's what I'm all about: keeping it real. Ain't no "mock" anything in my game, know what I'm saying? Now, what I need to know, baby doll, is, you want to see how fast I can be?

Nightmare

Begins with breaking glass, then unidentifiable, harrowing noises from downstairs, sounds stale, puce and rancid. A collective cacophony screaming malevolence, terrors, and agonies. Thuds and crashes swirl, creep their way to the stairwell, growing louder, suggestive, then identifiable. The elongated zip of whetstone across steel, the tearing of flesh, cries, calls and laughter deranged. Yelps of pain confirm the fate of the dog. Demonic laughter, dissonant drumming, and, baselining all other sounds, a fiendish *basso profundo* chant.

Her husband wakes and touches her arm. "Don't worry," he says. And because he is the rock upon which she built her church, her firewall against malevolence, terrors, and agonies, she is comforted, watches him stride to the top of the stairs, his chest full and hard, his shoulders broad, foundational.

Which makes the look he gives her all the more devasting. Horror mixed with incomprehension; revulsion and a hint of disgust. His eyes briefly flick toward the gun safe, then back down the stairwell. He knows he doesn't have time. The ghoulish horde, creeping up the steps, are legion, inexorable, and final. Individualized grotesques bubble above the surging shadows on the wall opposite the stairwell. A bestial vanguard excretes into view, then she wakes, shattered and hollow.

What haunts her that day (and all the days that follow)

was not the chanting, nor the discordant music accompanying it, nor the horrifying visages that flashed before that waking moment, but the look on her husband's face. A look of soul-deliquescing defeat. And of apology. Not for not being strong enough, but for allowing her to believe such a strength existed.

The Problem with Inspiration

Because sometimes the Muse is a bitch, moody, petty, passive-aggressive, won't return my calls, my texts.

What can I do in the face of this silence?

I can stare at the blank screen, empty of thoughts, while the cursor winks at me, in on some joke only it and the Muse knows.

I can stare out the window at the birds—for whom all of this seems to come so naturally—flit from branch to branch, like I'm Keats, or Coleridge (hell, I'd even settle for Hardy).

Or perhaps I just become pragmatic, literal, methodical, rely on nothing more exotic than the Rule of Three, make the poem plain, ponder the profundity of punctuation, make the poem a perfunctory pile up of wrestled words, a primer of 4th-grade English, nouns, verbs, adjectives (but not adverbs, fuck them!), something mechanical, sterile that even my engineer uncle can understand.

Because isn't that the real problem with Inspiration? Doesn't the very idea of the Muse suggest something cabalistic, mystical, that "elitist nonsense" my uncle would call it?

But maybe I just feel this way because I'm tired. Tired of

wrestling with words. Some of them can be damn ornery. Like "ornery," for example. Tired of the cursor mocking my emptiness. And don't even get me started on those fucking birds, flitting around so smug, so goddamnned superior.

Or maybe I'm just tired of waiting for Inspiration to call me, text me (even an DM on the Facebook would be something); so I can say, "I'm sorry"; so I can say, "please come home"; so I can say, "I love you," hope She says, "I love you, too"; hope She says "I'll never leave again"; so I can at least hear her voice, just one more time.

This Life Instead Of

Ronin

The single rain cloud hangs low and black like the dug of some fantastic beast. Behind it, blue sky promises only a delay, so we trot into our respective dugouts to wait it out. On the other side, First Methodist, the team I played for for the last three years. They glare at me in their mismatched shirts. "Turncoat," a few mutter as I jog by.

Recruited to switch teams this winter, to take one of the three spots allotted to non-church members, I am now a nominal Lutheran. Lyn, the Methodist captain, asks if I'll be playing for Presbyterian next year, cycling my way through faiths and teams until I find a home.

The rain pockmarks the infield, the smell of rinsed grass jostling that of leather. I sit on the back of the bench, using the seat to knock mud from my cleats. The rest of the team, in matching blue uniforms, gather around Pastor Steve in prayer. He's a nice guy, and seems beloved by his flock, but he's a shitty ballplayer, so I tune him out.

But when he ecstatically cries out and points to the sky, I can't help but look. Arching behind the cloud, a perfect rainbow, resplendent and glorious. "God has kept his promise," Pastor Steve calls out. "He shall not drown us in deluge."

I roll my eyes and chuckle, but then notice the rapture on the faces of the others. They believe this. They look up and see the rainbow as real promise. They do not see solely iridescence, but salvation, their ancient religion made contemporary and real.

To me, it only means the game can resume. I knock the last of the mud from my spikes, jog back out to the hot corner, grab a handful of wet dirt and grind it into my palms.

There are two outs. I'm due up third next inning.

Hermit

What does the crab feel, I wonder, as it leaves its old shell?
It was close and cramped, surely, or else why would he leave it?
But it was also safe, habitual.

And what of those moments in-between shells?
Does he feel liberated?
Released from the tight confines that stifled?
Or does he feel terribly-exposed?
Naked and unmasked?

What does he think of his new shell?
Does it excite him?
Does he see in it opportunities for new growth?

Or is it just a bigger place in which to hide?

Coward

We were discussing the Sudan in class,
the genocide and the Lost Boys,
my righteous indignation at our collective apathy,
when he asked the question:

"If this is so important, if this is so wrong, as you claim it is,
then why aren't you doing anything about it?"

His smugness a challenge,
I debated kicking him out of class.
Instead, I answered:

"Because I don't know what else to do,
and until I have a better answer, I'm telling *you*,
with the hope that you'll think of something better."

His face left no doubt about his measure of me,
In his eyes, I was a coward.

What does he know?
He's just young, naive, and unplugged.

PAUL JUHASZ

But when Trayvon Martin was assassinated, I simply shook my head in disgust,
I may have said something protesty at the dinner table.

When Eric Garner was choked to death,
left on the sidewalk like last week's trash,
I wrote an angry post on Facebook.

When Sandra Bland was arrested for driving-while-black,
her murder in a jail cell three days later whitewashed as suicide,
I made my profile picture her beautiful, smiling face.

When Trump was elected, I wrote a poem.

When this week's school shooting occurs, I'll hug my sons, and pray the lottery keeps passing us by.

I do these things not because I don't know what to do.
Or because I don't have a better answer.
I know what the right thing to do is.

But I hide within the privilege of whiteness,
Its comfort, its reflexive assumptions,
and I try to ignore the shame of not wanting to lose that.

But with every effete gesture, every paltry statement of indignation,

RONIN

I see the face of that smug student,
and I'm forced to recognize the truth:

I am a coward.
And so, I'm telling *you*.

Eighth Ring

They thought of everything here:

Guacamole long-since crusted and grey.
Forced conversations framed by silences
more agonizing than awkward.
IKEA furniture haphazardly-assembled.
Michael Bolton cycled and recycled, and recycled and
recycled and recycled interminably.
The cheap beer is warm and stale.
No candles in the bathroom, the door to which does not
 close.
All smells, sights, and sounds filtered through an atmosphere
 of
dog hair, ubiquitous and suffocating.
And the clocks, of course, are all broken.

Who knew Damnation could be so boring?

They Wave as They Drive By

Sometimes it's just two fingers, sometimes the whole hand, flared off the steering wheel as you pass each other on country roads. Never on Interstate, because it seems to require a narrowed-experience, a patina of community. And that's the thing that gets me: the assumptive kinship.

They don't do this on the coasts. The only wave you get there is the one-fingered kind, over-reactive and violent.

But not out here. Here, they wave as they drive by. They have no way of knowing I'm an outsider, a Yankee, a liberal, but I suspect it wouldn't matter; they'd wave anyway. Because before we're those other things, we're just people trying to get where we're going, flashing fellow-travelers, random vectors, sharing a fleeting moment and transitory space.

So I force myself to wave back.

Seven Tips for Uber-Riders: A Helpful Guide

Tip One: Let your driver select the best route to take.[1] Please remember that the obvious way is not always the fastest way.[2]

Tip Two: Avoid making eye-contact in the rearview mirror.[3] Yes, even if we're having a conversation.[4]

Tip Three: Respect the Uber driver's car at all times.[5]

Tip Four: Please don't say "Oops!" if your child throws up in my car.[6] Nor should you ask for a napkin while observing that "it's just a little bit."[7]

Tip Five: Always sit in the back seat[8]. If, for some reason, you feel compelled to sit in the front passenger seat, you better be prepared to have a conversation.[9]

Tip Six: My car, my music.[10]

Tip Seven: If the service was excellent,[11] please remember to tip your driver.[12] Please never say "I'll tip you on the app."[13]

---

1. I'm getting my directions from *space*. Remember that. From space! And even if satellites weren't helping me, I'd rely on my professional knowledge of the area roads. So, please do not say to me "Don't you think we should take Ave X or Y St?" If I did, I would be driving on Ave X or Y St, wouldn't I? In our momentary encounter, I am the professional, not you. When I'm

in your office, I don't say "Don't you think you should prescribe me an anti-depressant instead of a psychostimulant?" do I? A better way to spend your ride is to just sit back and pretend that you are so successful that you have your own private driver. Don't we all grow up wanting our own private driver? I'm sorry I don't have a chauffeur's hat, to make the illusion seem more real.

2. If you insist on always taking the obvious route, just understand that in a zombie apocalypse, you die before me.

3. And if you accidently make eye-contact, for the love of God, don't hold it. It's creepy and awkward. Unless, of course, I have The Righteous Brothers or Marvin Gaye on the radio. In which case, I'm trying to seduce you.

4. According to movies, you're supposed to look wistfully out the window when having a conversation with a stranger in a car, so let's roll with that. You and I are in a movie. But it's *your* movie, remember. I'm just a bit part. Probably don't even have a name in the credits. Just something like "Driver," or, if in your movie you want to strive for precision, perhaps "Uber Driver." Because this is your movie and I'm just a glorified extra, we should probably keep conversation to a minimum. Perhaps no more than a line or two. If that. Even better if we can just stick to gestures. You don't want to know me. That's why every fucking one of you starts a conversation asking "So, how long have you been driving for Uber?" It's reflexive, and hollow, and you don't care. I bet if I quizzed you at the end of the ride, you wouldn't remember my answer. But that's fine, because I don't want to know you either.

5. I am not a carny. I do not have a shoddily-crafted collection of stuffed animals to award as prizes. Therefore, please do not treat my trunk hatch as a midway game designed to test your strength. If you do this, understand that I will back the car up and run over your toes.

6. My car is my office. If I brought one of my sons to *your* office, and he dropped trou and left a Lincoln log on your desk, rest assured I'd say something more appropriate than "Oops!"

7. I have had children. It is NEVER just a little bit. The preferred reaction would be to shout "Holy shit, this is going to be expensive (a $200 clean-up fee no matter how many times you dab at the puddles with your precious napkin). Offers to procure latex gloves, hoses and/or Haz-Mat suits are also acceptable.

8. It's shockingly presumptuous to do otherwise. The front passenger seat is traditionally reserved for friends and family. You are neither.

9. Not that I really want one. But it's very creepy if you don't. To assume a familiarity but then remain coolly aloof. You know who does this? Psychopaths, that's who. If you stay silent in the front seat, I'm just going to assume you are a serial killer getting a ride to work. I keep a corkscrew under my seat for such occasions, and I'll stab you in the throat the first chance I get, cut your body into pieces with a chainsaw (in a bathtub for ease of cleaning), dump half of the pieces in various local Dumpster, vacuum-seal the other pieces and UPS them to randomly-selected Chipotle restaurants, domestic and international.

10. Although, now that I think of it, this may be a bit strong. My musical boundaries have been expanded so much from suggestions by complete strangers, ones with the Flobots pouring from their headphones, the solemn ones who Bluetooth my stereo to fold themselves into St. Vincent. Maybe, I think to myself at these moments, music is a beautiful way for us to connect, to realize we could have conversations, play bigger roles in each other's movies, show compassion for sick children and respect for property. Until you play Maroon Five. Then I no longer think these things, and begin to lightly finger the corkscrew.

11. "Excellent" is to be understood as "you were delivered to your destination safely and in a timely manner. And at no point did we try to kill each other." Isn't that the best one can hope for these days?

12. We have long been told 1) do not get into a stranger's car, and 2) do not meet someone you've only met online. You've just done both. It was a foolish thing to do. You put yourself in peril. Of course, by picking up a stranger, I've put myself in peril too. So here we are, two strangers randomly thrown together, both masking the unease and desperation of contemporary human interactions under a veneer of normalcy and social advancement. We pretend it's cool, but we know it's not. We pretend we're friendly, but we know (perhaps hope) we'll never see each other again. A tip bridges this divide, is a moment of human-to-human contact. Tips do NOT need to be monetary. A genuine smile, an honest question, the answer to which has attention and interest paid, a breath mint. These are also tips.

13. We both know this is a lie. All you are really saying here is that you accept this world we've created, and are unwilling, for one brief moment, to cross the gulf between us, to connect. You're saying that you've embraced the void as just and right and real. Know that I will hate you for that. Who knows what we may have been?

Masturbators

Grandma, scowling, referred to it as "that nasty habit of yours." Dad would just smirk and ask what I was doing in the bathroom for so long; Mom would wrinkle her nose and warn that I would have to start washing my own socks.

But when Mrs. Grinshaw mentioned it during her history lesson, I was more than a little surprised. Not because she used the word, but the implications it suggested. Really? Stephen Douglas did it? Abe Lincoln too? For once, my daydreams did not involve luscious Suzy Sanders, seated across the aisle, with her short skirt and her hair ribbons. Lincoln and Douglas. Great men. Great men who, apparently, hamstrung their potential for greatness by indulging in this deplorable act.

Is that why Douglas's political career got stuck at the state level? Was a national voting public unable to look past his hairy palms? Did blindness prevent Lincoln from seeing a crouching, stalking Boothe? Would I meet them both in Hell, where Grandma was so confident I'd end up because of my own energetic self-defilement?

But then Mrs. Grinshaw said it again, and this time I heard her more clearly: "Lincoln and Douglas were both master debaters." Alone once again with my shame, I turned my attention back to Suzy Sanders, memorizing her every curve, her creamy thighs, the promise of breasts, those taunting hair ribbons, and hoped that when I thought of her later that night, she would not appear in a stovepipe hat, or with a Shenandoah beard.

I Was Trying to Write a Poem

I was trying to write a poem this morning when you joined me on the deck. I guess from inside the house I looked like I was just taking in a moment filled with sunrise, birdsong, and human silence. But I wasn't. I was trying to write a poem, for which I've found sunrise, birdsong, and human silence quite helpful. But then you showed up. Wanting to talk. Something about if it was possible to love two people at once. Which, of course, it is. Not only possible, but desirable. Love as many people as you can, as deeply as you can. Try not to rank them (although, this, admittedly, is not always possible). I didn't say this to you this morning, because I was trying to write a poem. I think instead I said something clichéd, something that made it seem like I was listening, but of course, I wasn't. But now, looking back at your poem-interruption, I realize that even if I had said all of this, that was not what you wanted to hear. You wanted *permission* to love someone else and of course, that I can't give you. Poems, sometimes, give that permission. But I didn't get to write *any* poem, let alone the permission-to-love-someone-else kind, so that sucks for you.

    I was trying to write a poem right before lunch when your wife joined me on the deck. I guess from inside the house I looked like I was pondering parts of the conspiratorial conversation she saw you and I have this morning. She went on and on about the local flora and fauna she likes to observe from the deck (you know, the deck where I was trying to write a poem). Honey suckle this, red-breasted that, on and on. What she really wanted to talk about, I now realize, was you. She's not an idiot, she senses something is up. Although, since she was pointing out beautiful birds like warblers and cardinals, not birds that rend and tear like hawks and gulls, I'm of the mind that she does not have a real clear picture of what's going on, that you love someone else. I probably should have said something about this, and about how you still love her as well and that's where the doubt and confusion that makes us all so wonderfully human comes in. But I said nothing. First, because I was annoyed that she interrupted the writing of my poem. Second, because it's not my fucking job, is it? You should be telling her these things instead of interrupting my serious poem writing.

I was trying to write a poem this afternoon when you came back onto the deck. Seriously!?! I guess from inside the house I looked like I was trying to figure out how I was going to be the go-between for you both. But I don't want to be a go-between. I just want to write this goddamn poem! You started asking me if she knew you had fallen in love with someone else and all I could think of is how you two were made for each other. Mr. and Mrs. Poem Interrupter. I realize now that what you were really trying to say was that the last thing you want to do is hurt her. Because you still love her. Deeply. But you love someone else deeply as well. And you have to be true to that and to yourself. I realize now I should have said something like "It's not necessary to gauge which love is deeper, that life takes care of that for you. You have no idea where these paths lead, so for now just revel in this bounty of deep love you have and be open to whatever path ultimately presents itself." That may not be the best expression of the idea, of course. I could have, perhaps, expressed it more beautifully if people did not keep interrupting me when I'm writing poems.

I was trying to write a poem this evening when Johnny Jr. joined me on the deck. I guess from inside the house it didn't look like I wasn't doing much of anything. He came out and told me of a bad dream he had last night. It involved a crack on the ground that kept getting larger. He had one foot on each side of the crack and was getting stretched as the crack expanded. When he looked down into the fissure, he saw a giant dragon with its mouth wide open, ready to eat him. Your son was scared he would have the same dream again tonight. I realize now he was saying he was worried about you and your wife. Kids aren't stupid. They can sense when things aren't quite balanced. I probably should have told him that everything would be OK. That love is complex, but it is that complexity that makes it beautiful. The problem, I would have continued, is that many people forget this about love. They make love into something divisive, exclusive. They sharpen its edge and make a weapon of it. But there are people out there (we'll call them poets, Johnny) whose job it is to remind the others what love is all about. If they're left alone, that is.

I'm tired. And beaten down by all the interruptions. I've

resigned myself to the fact that I will not get a poem written today. And that's too bad. I was planning on writing a great love poem. But then you, and then your wife, and then you again, and then your kid, messed all that up. Maybe if I'm lucky the poem I was trying to write will come back to me in the liminal zone that precedes sleep. Maybe I'll dream of the poem. Perhaps I'll find it in the dragon's mouth. And if I do, I'm not going to wait for the morning, for sunrise and birdsong, to write it. That way, when you or your wife or Johnny come out onto the deck, we can have an uninterrupted conversation. About love. Or anything else.

I, Sherrett

It was just a simple statement of synergy, talk-to-text assurance that, regarding my wife's view on some minor, now forgotten subject, we were *simpatico*. But some goblin—the same, no doubt, responsible for vandalizing other attempts at hands-free communication, twisting promises to mow the yard "Saturday Norm," or distorting the catalog of my day with the declaration that I ate lunch at the new "tie compliment"—this goblin, I say, this perverse imp has garbled my "I share it" statement of solidarity into "I Sherrett."

At first, I was annoyed at this desecration of my consolation, but then, what if this was something else? Not a mistake but an existential declaration? An alter-ego? My Mr. Hyde, my Batman.

Or even better: Sherrett as scapegoat, as pariah. Perhaps I was not responsible for my many failings; Sherrett was. It was not I, Paul, who forgot to lift the toilet seat, to grab a gallon of milk on the way home. It was not I who may or may not have killed the neighbor's cat (just to see what it felt like); who failed to be a better husband, father, friend, neighbor. It was Sherrett! Shame on you, Sherrett!

Then my thoughts turned dark, the statement on my phone menacing, erasing. Technology trumping identity once again. Siri has long ignored my humanity, subverting even the most carefully-worded requests, answering my query about MLB scores with a list of stores selling emerald coats. Or brushing me off with a "here's what I found on the Internet," her polite way of telling me to fuck off and not bother her. Each new online account declares I cannot be Paul or "pjuhasz." I can only be "pjuhasz145." To my bank, I am just four numbers; the Xbox knows me as "Category Five" and Facebook says I am any one of several algorithmically-determined characters from *Star Wars, Harry Potter, Lord of the Rings,* or *Game o Thrones.* And now my phone was telling me I was Sherrett. I do not want to be Sherrett.

Perhaps a third option: Sherrett as chrysalis. A chance to leave a Clark Kent cocoon behind, an abandoned husk of nearly fifty-years of character flaws, mistakes large and small, a world of disappointments, false-starts, "Cease and Desist" letters, and dead ends, all erased by a rebirth, not in Christ, but in Apple.

My phone chimes. I glance at its face. A text from my wife: "Who the fuck is Sherrett?" I breathe deep, stretch and flex my body, enjoying a new-found litheness. Perhaps it's time she knew: "I, Sherrett."

Pulling Weeds

My impatient friends are right, of course. They will just grow back. Crabgrass, chickweed, buckhorn plantain, the inexorable quack grass, all will be back, encroaching, metastasized, choking the small square flower bed we plant around the mailbox each spring. Always petunias. Some years, a comingling of purples and whites—our wedding colors. Other years, clearly bifurcated regions of whatever color struck our individual eyes as we separately walked the greenhouse.

"It's not even your house anymore," Jason says, anxious to get to the bar for our one last hurrah. "Yeah," Bryan adds, "let her pull her own fuckin' weeds." And, of course, they're right about that too. It is her house now. Tomorrow morning, I'll pull away in a laden U-Haul, a quit claim to the life we've built over two decades.

But that's not what matters.

One last Saturday afternoon, my boys will come back from the park and see me working, sweating. Some of this soil will remain under the fingernails that will grip the steering wheel tomorrow's dawn. For a short while she can look out the bedroom window and think about a time resplendent.

Weeds will always grow back. That's the unavoidable truth about gardening. In the beds you share and in the ones you leave behind. So you pull them out when they do.

Beard

I'm growing it this time because my sons asked me too. They want to see what Dad looks like with one. They think I'll look cool. Like those post-apocalyptic survivors they see on TV and in movies. Like NHL players making deep playoff runs. I know better. I've tried before. It will be just a patchwork, a failed mosaic. Scrubland of black and white. Like the flame-scoured hills of the Yellowstone, charred black trunks next to dead white ones. Embarrassing. Shameful. Something that will never be whole, never be full, always falling short.

All the men in my family have beards. Rich, full beards. They compare length, adorn them with clever names like Flavor-Saver and Thigh-Tickler. They grill blocks of *szalona*, laugh over their Scotch, share stories of successful hunts. The spotting, the tracking, and the move in for the kill. Of deer, elk, women. Brag about stats: eight-point and 36D racks. They are men. They stroke their lush, luxuriant beards. They laugh at my lack of one; they wonder at my inability to grow one.

My uncle has a beard. A rich, full one. He had an illegitimate daughter he never recognized. She died of a heroin overdose. At the news, my uncle said "Fuck her!" He once intentionally stepped in front of a car, collecting a sizable insurance settlement and a lifetime of Disability checks. He lied, stole, cheated. He told my wife that he had a massive cock and she should call him some night for an introduction to it. He has a beard, lush and luxuriant. He laughs at my lack of one.

My cousin has a beard. A rich, full one. He blasts his shotgun at the neighbors' house when he thinks the music is too loud. He abuses his four-year-old granddaughter. Pinches her until she cries. The tears make him stronger. Amuse him. He beats his wife. Drives her deeper into alcoholism. He has a beard, lush and luxuriant. He laughs at my lack of one.

My father has a beard. A rich, full one. We played a game when I was a boy. Lift the Arm. A game of his own invention. Simple rules. I punch him in his arm one hundred times; he punches me in mine once. Then we would see who could lift their arm. The rub: he got to go first. "Go on," he would encourage me after slugging me with all his might, "lift your arm." When I could not, he would crow "I guess I win then." He had a thing for Puerto Rican prostitutes. Cost him his marriage. A price he seemed more than happy to pay. He has a beard, lush and luxuriant. He wonders at my inability to grow one.

I detest *szalona*. I don't drink Scotch. I don't hunt. I'm growing this beard now because my sons asked me too. They want to see what Dad looks like with one. They think I'll look cool. Like those post-apocalyptic survivors they see on TV.

I know better. I've tried before. But I also know every now and then, I'll try to grow one again. If only so I can shave it off.

Bartholomew Cubbins Tries Psychoanalysis

The rack behind the office door is overwhelmed, its paltry four hooks no match for the avalanche of hats. Derbies, porkpies, fedoras, a bearskin, *un sombrero*, a dusty *akubra*, berets, a tattered and worn Chicago Cubs cap, a pith helmet, stovepipes, half a dozen *kufi*, a pierced Hardee rumored to have once decored the head of Colonel Sturgis at Little Big Horn, a flaccid *chullo*, and topping the pile, like the cherry on top of a haberdashic sundae, a single, bright-red *fez*.

The office itself is quite drab, more academic than clinical. Full of serge, paisley, and corduroy. Sitting in a green chair next to the couch is Dr. Freud himself, a cutout from the fabric of the room. A scrub of white hair on a balding head, the meticulously-trimmed beard, a cigar—which is just a cigar—nestled in his right mouth-point. He chews it absent-mindedly, confident his patient, who, after all, is just a character from a children's book, will excuse this minor unprofessionalism. As he takes notes, he caresses the epithelioma in his cheek.

"Tell me, Mr. Cubbins, about your mother."

"It occurs to me," the patient replies after a moment's thought, "that at the exact moment of my birth, I was wearing her as a hat. And that seems to have made quite an impression."

Barn Cat

The problem with barn cats is that none of it is genuine. When the cat runs to me in excitement every morning, it's just because I usually have food. More food than you're supposed to give to a barn cat, according to my friends. But it's not *real* affection. And the seductive purring, the passionate rubbing against your leg, all of it, is nothing more than the fondness one feels for a favorite waiter.

Of course, I know this. Know this as I begin shopping at Petco, know this when I think how nice it would be if the cat was inside tonight, curled up beside me on the couch, know this when I get up fifteen minutes early, just to spend some time with the cat before I go to work.

I know all of this. But I also know I'll miss her when she stops showing up. I know that until that day, I'll hope and I'll dream, will be there every morning to feed, to stroke, to share. Because it doesn't matter if her affection was just for show, was just about survival. What matters was that mine was real.

Because I'm A White Man

God damn, it's great to be a white man!

Because I'm a white man, I get to grab 'em by the pussy, and become President.

Because I'm a white man, I can say "it's heritage, not hate."

Because I'm a white man, cops won't shoot me during traffic stops.

Because I'm a white man, the Second Amendments is exclusively my own.

Because I'm a white man, I get to say "there are some good Nazis."

Because I'm a white man, I get to cheer for the Washington Redskins.

Because I'm a white man, I get to rape women and become a Supreme Court Justice.

Because I'm a white man, I get to indignantly ask, "Why do they get to say 'nigger,' but I can't?"

Because I'm a white man, I get to shoot up schools, malls, gay nightclubs, mosques and churches.

Because I'm a white man, I get to pretend that rights are like pie; if others get some, there's less for me.

Because I'm a white man, I get to hope cancer takes out Ruth Bader Ginsburg.

Because I'm a white man, I get to act like I don't understand, when really, I just don't give a shit.

Because I'm a white man, I recognize I am part of the problem, whether I like it or not.

Because I'm a white man, I know that a good Nazi, like a leprechaun or the Tooth Fairy does not exist.

Because I'm a white man, I understand that if you grab 'em by the pussy; you're not the greatest president ever, nor are you a messiah, you're just a piece of shit.

Because I'm a white man, I understand it's not a fucking pie!

Because I'm a white man, I understand that the reason they get to say that word is because after centuries of denigration and dehumanization, they are claiming that word as theirs, recasting it on their own terms, and they do not need my permission, nor are they asking for my opinion.

Because I'm a white man, I understand my silence is complicity.

Because I'm a white man, I understand the solution must start with me.

Because I'm a white man, I get to teach my sons that whiteness and maleness are nothing more than accidents of birth.

Because I'm a white man, I get to teach my sons that the world is full of their brothers and their sisters.

Because I'm a white man, I get to teach my sons to not be silent.

Because I'm a white man, I get to teach my sons to be better.

God Damn, it's great to be a white man!

Just Missed

I kneel down on the chessboard-patterned floor of the mall food court, noticing my shoe laces are untied. It will take me somewhere between 2-5 seconds to retie them.

Two seconds means I miss colliding into that man wearing a light-blue windbreaker despite the searing August heat. He's a serial killer, concealing an axe-blade fresh from the whetstone in his pocket. An axe blade he will now bury into the skull of someone other than me.

Three seconds ensures I do not strike up a conversation with William, an entrepreneur looking for a partner, waiting in line at Panda Express two people (now) in front of me. When his start-up goes public, he will be on the cover of *Forbes*. I will still be putting bottles of vitamins into padded envelopes.

At four seconds, I miss the drunk driver running a red light on my drive home. Instead, he will crash into a Honda Odyssey, killing a young mother and one of her daughters. The surviving daughter will resent it when her father re-marries. Her step-mother, however, will encourage the daughter's talent for painting, will beam proudly at her first exhibit at the Robert Klein Gallery.

Five seconds costs me a meeting with Heather, who would have been sitting at my usual table at the Starbucks three blocks from my apartment, where I will drink my white chocolate mocha alone, not aware that Heather was the woman I was supposed to marry.

The shoe once again tethered, I go order my General Tso's with fried rice, then walk to Bed, Bath and Beyond, where I will buy a mirror for the bathroom, living this life instead of myriad others, a boundless parcel of lives just missed.

Beautifully, Impossibly, In Flight

Vectors

My sons cannot stop laughing at it. Over and over again they watch the YouTube clip. Randy Johnson. The Big Unit. A 6'10" freak of nature, foreboding on a raised patch of dirt. Unkempt hair greases down his face and head as he glares at the nothing in the batter's box. A few blinks of intimidation, and Johnson uncurls his lankiness, snakes out his left arm, and delivers. The heater, the gas, the Number One.

Johnson's fastball regularly clocked in over 100 mph. So devastating, so terrifying that at one All-Star game, John Kruk stepped out of the batter's box when Johnson went into his wind-up. You can read his lips: "Nope. Fuck this." Three pitches later, he was back on the bench, out but safe, alive.

No such luck on March 24, 2001. Johnson fires off the pitch, and a blink later, an explosion of feathers. The ball never reaches the plate, the forgotten batter forfeited by the most improbable, the most amazing confluence of trajectories. A bird. A perfectly-timed dove, disintegrates into nothingness, an event for which there is no cabalistic notation in the minutiae of baseball scorekeeping.

I understand my sons' laughter. I do. For laughter is a common response to the amazing, the unbelievable, and if you've seen this clip, you know it is truly one of the most unbelievable things ever. Randy Johnson just hit a dove with a fastball. Hit it with such precision, such force, that there's only a handful of feathers to prove that a blink before, a dove existed. He has, in essence, erased it. This fact overwhelms one with the impossibility of its possibility. This particular collision of vectors is unbelievable precisely because it happened.

And this is where my reaction to the video clip differs from that of my sons. They are still young, still caught up in the novelty of experience. The clip to them is new. But I saw it eighteen years ago, have had that time to process its implications. It's a *memento mori*, certainly; a reminder that somewhere out there is a bullet, a cancer, a drunk driver on its own vector, barreling its way towards yours, towards mine. But for me, the essence of this event something else. It's the way Johnson's arm traces a question mark in the air as he throws his pitch. And it's the fact that before the collision, that dove is beautifully, impossibly, in flight.

Not All Who Wander Are Lost

It's alright, you can look me in the eye. I know it ain't you personally. Just doing your job. If it helps, don't think of it as "running me off" ('cause I can see in your eyes that's how you see this). I don't see it that way. We's just moving on, Bessie and I, and I invite you to see it that way too. This here's a grand country to be moving on in.

It's alright, you can look me in the eye. Most people don't, can't or won't. Never been too sure which. The ones who give and the ones who pretend I'm invisible. 'Cept when I tell them I ain't after their money, don't want a handout. Ha! That always gets me a flick up into my eyes to see if I'm joking, proud, or just plum crazy. Ain't neither, by the way, if you wuz wondering. I do ok, I suppose. 'Course I ain't opposed to someone gittin me a cup of coffee, like you did here, (and I thank you kindly for that). Always nice to drink something warm on a chill morning like this one. Or when they have something for Bessie. I do appreciate that too. She still has some wolf in her somewheres, I think, but I don't s'pose she's opposed to a can of Alpo now and again.

It's alright, you can look me in the eye (and you can use this here kerchief of mine if you'd like). Problem you have, officer, if you don't mind my saying it, is binary. Right or wrong, legal or illegal, trash or food, homeless or housed. Those ain't the only options. I'd take a warm Texas breeze, the smell of cedar and sage, of persimmon, the open vistas, over your cookie-cutter suburban house any day. S'pose there's some wolf left in me too. Sure, when it rains, I sometimes think it'd be nice to be dry, but other times, I don't. And the winters they got in some places can be a bit problem-matical. But like I said earlier, this here's a grand country to be moving on in. They's got these there trees up in California, bigger'n anything. I tell you, to see dawn filter through those branches, well, it ain't like nothing you ever saw. They got swamps in Florida and Georgia, just teeming with life, there's the Great River, black rolling hills atopping the plains. And mountains. I tell you son, I never get tired of them mountains, astride and laughing at us, sometimes good-naturedly, sometimes the other'n.

It's alright, brother, you can look me in the eye. Bessie and I are doing just fine.

Essential Oils

Yesterday, my wife received a package from Amazon. A diffuser, and a package of six vials of liquid the packaging indicated were "essential oils": peppermint, eucalyptus, lavender, cinnamon, lemongrass, and something called tea tree.

I spent a few moments wondering what the hell a tea tree was. Then I was grabbed by a larger question: if there were such things as "essential oils," didn't that presuppose a group of "inessential oils"? What oils, I wondered, were expendable, were not worthy of a diffuser or of a grandiose label?

Petroleum came immediately to mind, but I dismissed that as unrealistic. Labelling it "inessential" is really just wishful thinking and, if I'm being honest, betrays a political agenda. And the wags out there will be quick to point out that some jellies derived from petroleum oil have a certain zesty relevance.

I think we can all agree the world would be a better place without Crisco, so there's one.

I can hear the gourmands defending peanut oil, no doubt building their argument on its high smoking point. I once bough a bottle of peanut oil. In 1996. Twelve ounces of high smoking-point peanut oil. I *still* have about 11.9 ounces left. Hardly "essential."

I found a bottle in our kitchen cupboard with a tannish

oil in it, and a hand-written label identifying it as argan oil. Not only do I not know what argan oil is, I don't know whose hand-writing is on the label. Inessential for sure.

But then I started thinking once more about those "essential oils." Were any of *them* truly "essential"? I've known my wife for almost a quarter century, and for all but one day of that time, she seemed to do just fine without a diffuser spitting out essence of lemongrass. If you can go that long without something, how can it be essential?

But then, what is essential? Thoreau incites his readers to simplify, to strip life down to the essentials. And for years, I have been telling people *Thoreau* is essential. Would tell them I divide my life into two sections, before I read *Walden* and after I read *Walden*. "Why, then, did you name your son Emerson?" they ask. Thoreau, it appears, is not *that* essential.

Before sleep tonight, I ask my wife to turn on the diffuser, suggest we go with the peppermint, and as I drift off, I ponder the myriad mysteries of life, like "what is a tea tree?" "Why *didn't* we name him Thoreau?" and a thousand and sundry other questions, all of them, at their core, essential.

He Prefers Not To

Our father always liked to boast that since it was a brand-new development when all four families moved in there was a close bond between them all. "A real spirit of community," he would declare. Of course, the orgies probably helped, too. Initially, they were held outside, at one of the pools, until it became clear some of the older kids would watch from an upstairs bedroom. After that, they were moved indoors.

But if the four couples thought the change in location would outwit the voyeuristic curiosity of their children, they were mistaken. The night the party was held at the Wigerts, both Wigert boys snuck to the head of the stairs, peeped through the stairwell's wooden slats (designed to protect children from falling), and later reported to us all that they saw.

But what grabbed the neighborhood kids' interest this time was not the usual "who was with whom," nor the catalog of positions, nor the novelty of some unexpectedly-revealed perversion, but the odd behavior of Mr. Wigert, who apparently had decided at some point during the festivities that he no longer wished to participate. He spent the orgy, reportedly, sitting naked on the couch with his hands crossed over his privates, merely watching, like his two sons on the stairwell, the action in front of him.

The neighborhood children found this laughable and pathetic. But we were kids and knew no better. How noble, Mr. Wigert! How tragically selfless. So uncomfortable with the group dynamic, yet so unwilling to intrude on everyone else's fun. So he sat there, exuding a sense of shame they seemed incapable—or perhaps just unwilling—to share. It took three more orgies for Mr. Wigert to win his point.

 Ah, Wigert! Ah, humanity!

Usually

If I have something already in my hand when I see a spider, I usually kill it. The jerk of an elbow, the whack of magazine or hammer or an orange against the wall, and just a brownish smear remains.

But if I'm unarmed, I usually run from the room, usually screaming, sometimes crying, and then my wife, my brave, heroic wife, will go in and kill it. Usually it only takes her a half an hour to calm me down.

Usually, I try to explain the basis of my fear, but she hushes me. She knows already. She understands that ever since my sister dumped a mason jar of spiders over my head when I was six, I'm an acute arachnophobe.

But today, something *unusual* happened. I went into our bathroom to shave and saw a spider on the wall. Surprisingly, I had no impulse to kill it, nor did I run away. Instead, I just looked at it. *Really* looked at it. I spent a good minute or so in silent contemplation of its beauty. A mild, faded yellow, with hints of blue and green on its torso (or is it an abdomen? Or do they have backs?).

Perhaps because it had been climbing *up* the wall, which prevented me seeing its thousands of monster eyes or its blood-dripping fangs, or perhaps because the blue and green along its torsobackdomen had the luster of unpolished gemstones, I experienced a moment of tranquility. Of pure peace. As if the spider was patting me on the shoulders, three legs per side, as saying "There, there."

I would have petted it, but I threw up in my mouth a little at the thought. So, instead, I completed my morning ablutions with a smile on my face. Serene. At peace.

Until the thwack of my wife's slipper against the wall shattered the silence. She smiled at me, confident, knowing this is what I wanted, what I needed, from her.

Usually.

This is Just to Say Something Else

Dear William,
    I needed those plums.
    P.S
        I want a divorce

Residue

There's an old Ranchero on the street with leather seats, and it's pristine. Not a scratch, no dirt not even a whisper of ash. Reflective black, with red and yellow flame racing stripes. The rubble of the town lay strewn about the car. Cinder block, shards of glass, a kaleidoscope of torn fabrics, and of course, ash. Ubiquitous, deep, and pallid ash. The only color in the landscape three flickering letters on a neon sign reading "Eat at A**n**drew's **D**iner" and the car. Not permanent.

Just more permanent than the rest.

Wisdom

My son asks me "What rhymes with orange?"
"No, it doesn't" I answer.

"What month has 28 days" he asks.
"All of them," I reply.

A V of geese fly overhead, "Do you know what they call Canadian geese in Canada?" I ask.
"No."
"Geese."

Tonight, he shall dream of ash while I stay awake, wondering if the bathroom faucet is crying or is merely uninspired.

The Last Glove I Will Ever Buy

It's been coming for years, this moment. I've long joked that you can tell the age of a softball player by the number of braces he wears. Like tree rings, each brace represents a year past forty.

I wear seven, now. Two on each ankle, one per knee, and an arm sleeve, to prevent my elbow from flying off my body when I throw across the diamond.

Of course, I could stop. Could choose to interpret last August's playoff game, when a line drive tore through my glove's webbing, as a sign that it was time to hang 'em up. Wait a few years and join the Fifty-and-Over League. It's safer there, they tell me. I could accept defeat, and the slow roll towards old age, decrepitude, memory-loss, then death.

I think instead I will not go gently, not just yet. I'll buy the Wilson A-950, black leather with blue trim, on the rack before me, the glove the clerk assumes is for my son. I'll put my face deep into its 14" pocket and inhale the rich smell of leather and youth. I'll refuse the clerk's offer to use the steamer to break it in, preferring the more intimate way of oil and time. I'll buy Advil at Costco and put on my seven braces,

rub the infield dirt into my palms, inhale the newly-cut grass, still dive for line-drives down the line, still believe I can get to them, still believe I'll make the throw across the diamond, still believe,
for a just a little while longer.

Wisdom, Continued

"What's brown and sticky?" I ask my son the following morning.
"Don't know. Don't care," he replied.
"No, really, What's brown and sticky?"
"I don't know. What?"
"A stick."
He groans.

"Hey," I say as we have breakfast, "did you hear they're not making bananas any longer?"
"What? Really?"
"Yup. They decided bananas are long enough."
"Stop, Dad. Please. Stop."

I chose to ignore what sounds like anger in his voice.
"Two clowns are eating a cannibal," I say.
His face brightens. He gives me the smirk of the victor.
"One turns to the other and says, 'Does this taste funny?'"
He crows in delight at the stolen punch line.

"You're not listening," I say. "Two *clowns* are eating a *cannibal*. One turns to the other and says 'I think we have this joke wrong.'"
His eyes crush down, his defeat manifest.
But then he smiles, nodding in complete, perfect, understanding.

Paper Thin

For Shannon.

There is a piece of paper. Onto this piece of paper, you tattooed your secrets. Words of rage, defiance, fear, and pain. You think your piece of paper is special (and it is) and is uniquely you (and it is), but I wonder about your claim that the difference with your piece of paper is that it is about you, and not me. Is that true?

I also have filled pieces of paper with words of rage, of defiance, of fear, and of pain. Sometimes, those words are strikingly similar to the ones you use. Sometimes I read your piece of paper and think it describes me. Sometimes I read your piece of paper and know it is you. Sometimes I read your piece of paper and think it's both of us, simultaneous.

So, you see, your piece of paper *is* still a piece of paper. A sliver of tree onto which you begin your thoughts and end your conclusions. But it is also something else. Something beautiful, something magical. Your piece of paper is a conduit. Through it, I can take your hand, shake it or hold it, as need requires; through it, we embrace, re-connected for the first time; through it, I hear your voice; through it, we share a world, a world where—despite the constant insertion of barriers and walls and laws and religions and labels and definitions and identities—the distinction between a you and a me is as thin as this piece of paper.

Cocoon

Shattered slivers of sanctuary surround,
still mucus-slick and warm,
as it pauses on the branch,
letting the sun's warmth dry
the new vibrancy.

What came before fades,
its hold loosens to irrelevancy,
leaving just the
remurgance.
and the subsequent unleashing
of flight.

Gestalt

Pebbled mosaic litter the floors of tollbooths masquerading as catacombs. Sticky cinema floors fetishize the flight of rumored birds. Deciduous gales rape street corners and marketplaces while mittens recall devoured fingers that haunt. Tides sharpen stained-glass saints, their reflective madness made glorious, grouped gazes spiraling toward this near-perfect truth: in lorazepam dreams, it is the ox that is not welcome. Junior varsity demons schedule professional-development classes, asking their sensei, "Is this quicksand?" On the mountain-tops, where the gilded gherkin-men live, bubble-wrapped scraps whisper of conch shells. Derelict Atari consoles dream of Wimbletons and percussion caps, red mist and manifestos. Meanwhile, in a corner where a howling silence demands to be made whole, brain-weary and headached children struggle to recall generational maxims. The world, voluptuously-gangrenous, built on the notion that, no matter the heuristic and in complete disregard of ordinals, the snail is always at home.

Oklahoma, Considered

David Foster Wallace tells us to consider the lobster. And we should. But not for the reasons he says. Instead, we should marvel that this creature, this armored, weaponed monster from the deep is something we eat. How in the actual hell did that happen? How unaccountable that someone in the long-ago saw a lobster, hideous, bottom-feeding fiend, and said "I'm going to draw some butter and eat that motherfucker," rather than worrying about the safety of his children, of his friends and family, of his very soul.

And while we're on the subject, consider bleu cheese? How did *that* happen? At least the lobster is an animated, living thing. But bleu cheese? A disk of piebald rot. Who the hell first thought, "I wonder if that festering circle of decay is tasty?" It must have been a bet; a "hold my beer and watch this" moment.

Or consider the coconut. Such a perfect food, really. The antioxidant-rich water inside is perfect for re-hydration, the milk silky and rich. If you chip off a piece of its wooly shell, you can use that as a utensil to scrape out the coconut's luscious meat. The coconut, when you consider it, is a self-contained place setting. A perfect nugget the world has created to feed us. And then placed in a tree 70 feet tall with no branches.

There is instruction in such things: The world will nourish

in unanticipated forms, in unpredictable ways, at unexpected times. This lesson strikes me as I stand beneath an endless sky and consider Oklahoma. After a twenty-two-year marriage has been drained of all love, as I stand exiled from an old garden in search of a new, I do not marvel that it is *this* land I'm drawn to. Not New Haven, where I was born and raised; not Texas, where I lived for fifteen years, not Pennsylvania, the false Eden from which I'm banished, but Oklahoma, a land I've visited maybe a dozen times at most.

Here, the wind acknowledges suffering, whispers healing and defiance. I will fill my lungs with it. Here, the warmth enfolds, embraces, rejuvenates. I shall let it burn my skin. Here, the red earth absorbs pain like a sponge. I shall offer it my sweat, take it beneath my fingernails. Here, I sense a spirit. I nod to It, and It nods to me. "Be at peace," It tells me, and I let that peace flow through me, filling me with hope, erasing doubt until the only question left to consider is:

Where in Oklahoma can I get a good lobster? In a coconut-cream sauce, with bleu cheese on my salad.

First Lines

"All the girls were disappointments from the start."

That's the line she gave him. Now, he had to write a poem around that. Adding to the pressure, she had already written a poem from a first line he gave her. A poem that began "Chasing sunsets is not as glamorous as they told us; until you catch one." A poem beautifully laden with her hopes and with her fears.

For days, he struggled. What to do? How to respond?

Should he, for example, write a poem about the first time she kissed him? How she stood across the room from him, in profile, in silent conversation with herself? How, her decision made, she strode confidently across the room, closing the distance so fast he didn't have time to get nervous? About her hands framing his face and how with the touch of lip and tongue she gave him back himself?

Or should he write about how in his dreams she wears a flower in her hair? That if he could be granted one wish, it would be to watch her eyes open in the morning, savor the quiet peace of her sleepy smile? That she not only completes the puzzle, but is the picture entire?

The problem, of course, was that none of those could begin with the line "the girls were a disappointment from the start." The second option she gave him— "he cut class and instead went to the roof of the gym to smoke and sunbathe"—wasn't much better.

What he should do, of course, is just ignore the girls who were disappointments, ignore the smoking, sunbathing class-cutter, just write the poem within him, the one that says fog is beautiful, that a view is determined by the person it is shared with, that the earth shakes only one way.

But he also knew that much better than writing that poem *to* her would be living that poem *with* her, a shared life of endless first lines, around which they would write poems, beautifully laden with their hopes and with their fears.

Amazing Hot Dogs

So the marquee outside of Mutt's on 23rd St. declared. That's an awfully bold statement. Amazing. As in "provoking astonishment" and "causing great surprise and wonder." Are there really people in the world, who, when confronted with meat paste mixed with water, salt, and nitrates crammed into a casing, then boiled, grilled, or steamed, and placed on a bun, react "with great surprise and wonder," are actually *amazed*?

Don't get me wrong, I enjoy a tasty hot dog. Sometimes they are quite delicious. I've even had a few I would say were exceptional. But *amazing*? No, I'm afraid I can't go that far. The only amazing thing about hot dogs, to my way of thinking, is that someone could be amazed by them.

I mean, how fucking basic do you have to be, to be amazed by the hot dog? "Wow," I hear these simpletons say, "tubular meat on bread! Stunning! Wait, you put ketchup and mustard on it too? [explosive noise] Mind blown! And what is this relish of which you speak?" What must they think of salsa? Or, God forbid, a well-crafted hollandaise?

By the time I arrive at The Drake, five minutes past my reservation, I find that I cannot stop thinking about that marquee, nor of the people inside, biting into their buns, shaking their heads in astonishment.

But as the waiter runs through the specials, I smell freshly baked bread. Outside the window, the Oklahoma sky is resplendent with sunset, pinks, reds, and purples blended. I take a drink from a glass of ice-cold tap water (distractedly ordered instead of my usual Pellegrino). At a nearby table, a child laughs. I recognize pedagogy. It matters not whether I choose the salt-crusted branzino, the miso-glazed grilled salmon, or the swordfish in piquillo pepper cream sauce. Offerings unsatisfactory. Savorless and vacant.

I head back to the car, anticipating the classic, all-beef, frank. With extra relish.

Bucket List

- Hold hands under moonlight.
- Make snow angels.
- Visit Carlsbad Caverns again, but for the first time.
- Get a hot dog at Mutts in Oklahoma City (I hear they are *amazing*).
- Find a sequoia. Hug it. See if our hands can touch.
- Discover whether you fit perfectly in the cruck of my left shoulder or the right one.
- Go around the neighborhood at Christmas time, stealing all the Josephs from the nativity sets. We can bring them all to the school playground and set them up on the swings, the slide, and the monkey bars. Because if anyone deserves a night of unbridled play, it's Joseph.
- Check out the *aurora borealis*, our favorite colors, orange and green, intertwined.
- Photobomb our own pictures.
- Discover what wine goes with Cap'n Crunch.
- Rescue a dog from a local shelter.
- Sit together on a love seat. Silently. Sharing breaths, absorbing each other's unique sounds, smells, and textures. Saying nothing, because we already know what it

is we don't have to say. Every now and again, say it anyway.
- Visit Petra.
- Leave each other short notes in odd places, like in a sock or eyeshadow case. Make each fifth one oddly disturbing ("I took all the pickles and hid them at the Nike outlet").
- Try a new ethic food. Turkish, maybe, or Burmese.
- Send each other dumb text messages about how some object says "I love you." (grrrck, grrrck, grrrck, clfff—that's how a manual can opener says "I love you.").
- Buy a case of Lucky Charms and eat only the marshmallows. Put the cereal outside for birds, name each one that shows up.
- Live in Dijon for three weeks, act so the locals think we're Canadian.
- Stay up all night reading each other poetry, then argue about whether Rick should have let Ilsa go with Lazlo (Let's face it, Renault is a fairly crappy consolation prize). Briefly resent that our definitions of "true love" are not in perfect synchronicity, then read each other poems we think Rick and Ilsa would have read to each other. Wait for the sunrise.
- Bake together. With aprons. Aprons are essential. You can pick what we bake, but I must insist it includes frosting. I'll speak like Julia Child if you'd like.
- Find out what flavor jelly bean the neighbor's daughter

loves best. Fill their mailbox with that kind. Because we should not be the only ones this damn happy.
- Have a Nerf gun fight with complete strangers. Show them no mercy.
- Ask an employee at Bed, Bath, and Beyond to direct us to their "Beyond" section.
- Buy an atlas. I'll open it at random and you put your finger on the page. We'll then buy plane tickets and go there. Or, even better, let's rent a car. We can take turns introducing each other to new music, have those conversations you can only have on long drives, like what's the weirdest road kill you've ever seen? Or which TV dad would you sleep with if you had to? (Dan Conner from *Rosanne*, duh!), Or what would life be like if we had never met?
- Go to the drive-through at McDonald's; keep repeating that our order is "to-go" until they ask us to leave.
- Swim with manatees. I guess it doesn't *have* to be manatees. Any aquatic mammal would do. But there's just something about manatees. An unwarranted grace. They are so at peace with their bodies that they make me more comfortable with mine. But really, any aquatic mammal will do. Just as long as you're there. That's really all I want. All I've ever wanted. Even when I didn't know I wanted it.
- Wonder how we got here. And where we're headed next.

How to Write an Oklahoma Poem

Start with the red earth. You don't have to call it "earth" though. You can refer to it as clay, dirt, or dust if you like. But it has to be red. And it has to get under your fingernails. This is metaphoric. Signifying a connection to you and the land that is symbiotic. You could, I suppose, have the dirt adhere to your boots instead, but this is a weaker metaphor, one apt to be misconstrued. Better stick with the fingernails.

Put the wind in your poem. It can be a howling wind, a twisting wind, a soothing wind, as you prefer. Depending on the ideas you wish your poem to express, it can whip across or scour or scream down Oklahoma's red earth (see above). It can be cold or suffocating or nourishing; it can muss your hair, blow off your baseball cap, or engulf you in a warm em-brace. But that wind has hurtled its way all the way from Canada or Mexico just to be with you today, so the least you can do is include it in your poem.

There has to be a mention of the sky. What you do with the sky is, of course, up to you. You're the poet, after all. You can have clouds in it that roll or roil, in whatever hues you like. You can fill it with birds if you wish. You can even throw a tornado in it, although that tends to change, sometimes radically, the tone of a poem if you're not careful. But the one thing your sky must be is vast, endless even, with vistas that seem to promise more than they can give, even after they've given it.

Speaking of birds, your Oklahoma poem must have a scissortail in it. I'm sorry, but there's really no leeway on this one. Now before those poets with other aviary favorites get all up in arms, you are more than welcome to populate your poem with hawks or owls—and there is a short list of other acceptable birds one could choose. All I'm saying is you have to have a scissortail in it as well, even if you just throw it in the corner of your poem, like Icarus in that Breughel painting.

As for terrestrial matters, your poem should have buffalo in it as well. Whether a lot of buffalo or a single old bull, forlorn or majestic (or both) is up to you. And feel free to call them buffalo. Some pencil-head academic somewhere will write a paper highlighting your zoological ignorance, noting that "buffalo" refers to Old World species in Asia and Africa only distantly related to these thunderous beasts of the American plains, but that's ok. Academics need to write stuff too.

Pepper your poem with place names. Tahlequah. Tishomingo. Wetumka. Wewoka. Revel in the harmony of the words and in the depth of the voices who said them first.

But the most important step to writing an Oklahoma poem is to distill yourself into its lines, because when you do, when you let your soul run free within it, when you are no longer writing so much as you're translating, when First Principles are whispered through you, then, at its very core, the center where the spirit is fed, your poem pulses with the understanding that every poem written in this way is an Oklahoma poem.

Unfettered by
Ephemeral Fears

Exodus

Those in the cities were the first to leave. Exchanging their clothes for burlap robes, they filed out of the cities and towns in columns, saying nothing, seeing nothing. The farmers and those in rural areas soon followed in like uniform. Where there were cliffs, they funneled over the edge lemming-style; those near lakes and ponds marched until waterlogged robes pulled them down. Where there were no cliffs and no lakes, they made do with what they could find. The ghastly parade shuffled on for two weeks, until there was no one left excepting a few anchorites isolated in the mountains, a ronin in fruitless search for a new master, a lone census-taker, and a single window-washer. The ronin was the first of these to go. Unfettered from ephemeral fears about honor and shame; he embraces at long last the novelty of *seppuku*. The census-taker followed a day later, having lost the numbers to count even so few. The anchorites merely faded away into cloud and fog, leaving just the window-washer. Dutifully, he hoisted the scaffold up his assigned building with bucket, squeegee, and soap, cleaning its glass face, into which sunlight shone in resplendent silence.

Acknowledgments

Acknowledgements

With gratitude to the editors of the journals and anthologies where the following poems first appeared:

Bull Buffalo and Indian Paintbrush (The Poetry of Oklahoma): "Oklahoma, Considered"

Dragon Poet Review: "Coward" & "Visiting Fort Wagner"

Red River Review: "Masturbaters" & "The Hare Licks His Wounds" & "Upon Visiting the National WWI Museum"

Speak Your Mind: "Because I'm a White Man" *Vox Poetica:* "Just Missed"

Poet Quarterly: "Exodus"

Living what could be charitably called a nomadic life, Paul Juhasz was born in western New Jersey, grew up just outside of New Haven, Connecticut, and has spent appreciable chunks of life in the plains of central Illinois, in the upper hill country of Texas, and in the Lehigh Valley in Pennsylvania. Most recently seduced by the spirit of the red earth, he now lives in Oklahoma City. Believing visceral experience is the essential force behind imagination, he has worked at a warehouse fulfillment center, manned a junk truck, and driven for Uber, all to gather material and characters for his poetry, fiction, and creative non-fiction. *Ronin* is his first collection of poetry. His blue-collar memoir *Fulfillment:Diary of a Warehouse Picker*, also from Fine Dog Press, debuted in 2020.

www.ingramcontent.com/pod-product-compliance
Lightning Source LLC
Chambersburg PA
CBHW071418070526
44578CB00003B/605